Y0-BTU-218

The

BIBLE PROMISE BOOK

for

Singles

BARBOUR
PUBLISHING, INC.
Uhrichsville, Ohio

©MCMXCVII by Barbour Publishing, Inc.

ISBN 1-57748-162-3

All rights reserved. No part of this publication
may be reproduced or transmitted in any form or
by any means without written permission of the
publisher.

Published by Barbour Publishing, Inc.
P.O. Box 719
Uhrichsville, Ohio 44683
http://www.barbourbooks.com

 Member of the
Evangelical Christian
Publishers Association

Printed in the United States of America.

The
BIBLE
PROMISE
BOOK
for
Singles

TABLE OF CONTENTS

AGREEABLE

We all like to have things our own way. Learning to compromise with others is hard work, and yet the Bible tells us that we can accomplish nothing unless we learn to be in agreement with others. As important as this skill is, the Bible also makes clear that our relationship with God is one area that we should never compromise for others.

Can two walk together, except they be agreed? *Amos 3:3*

Be of the same mind one toward another. . . . *Romans 12:16*

Be ye not unequally yoked together with unbelievers: for what fellowship hath righteousness with unrighteousness? and what communion hath light with darkness?

And what concord hath Christ with Belial? or what part hath he that believeth with an infidel?

And what agreement hath the temple of God with idols? for ye are the temple of the living God. . .

Wherefore come out from among them, and be ye separate, saith the Lord, and touch not the unclean thing; and I will receive you,

And will be a Father unto you, and ye shall be my sons and daughters, saith the Lord Almighty. *2 Corinthians 6:14–18*

Again I say unto you, That if two of you shall agree on earth as touching any thing that they shall ask, it shall be done for them of my Father which is in heaven. *Matthew 18:19*

Behold, how good and how pleasant it is for brethren to dwell together in unity!

Psalm 133:1

Agree with thine adversary quickly, whiles thou art in the way with him; lest at any time the adversary deliver thee to the judge, and the judge deliver thee to the officer, and thou be cast into prison. *Matthew 5:25*

Do all things without murmurings and disputings. *Philippians 2:14*

BEAUTY

We live in a world that values physical, external beauty. We spend time and effort making ourselves look more attractive, and we tend to value the same quality in others. There is nothing wrong with looking attractive, but we need to remember that true beauty, the beauty that will last for eternity, is found on the inside of a person, and it comes only from the Lord. Whatever our physical appearance, as we open our hearts to Christ, others will see His beauty reflected in our lives.

He hath made every thing beautiful in his time: also he hath set the world in their heart, so that no man can find out the work that God maketh from the beginning to the end.   *Ecclesiastes 3:11*

And how shall they preach, except they be sent? as it is written, How beautiful are the feet of them that preach the gospel of peace, and bring glad tidings of good things!
Romans 10:15

So shall the king greatly desire thy beauty: for he is thy Lord; and worship thou him.
Psalm 45:11

. . .For the LORD seeth not as man seeth; for man looketh on the outward appearance, but the LORD looketh on the heart.
1 Samuel 16:7

And let the beauty of the LORD our God be upon us: and establish thou the work of our hands upon us; yea, the work of our hands establish thou it. *Psalm 90:17*

For the LORD taketh pleasure in his people: he will beautify the meek with salvation.
Psalm 149:4

One thing have I desired of the LORD, that will I seek after; that I may dwell in the house of the LORD all the days of my life, to behold the beauty of the LORD, and to inquire in his temple. *Psalm 27:4*

Favour is deceitful, and beauty is vain: but a woman that feareth the LORD, she shall be praised. *Proverbs 31:30*

BLAMELESS

As single Christians, we need to work hard to live blameless lives, for we are Christ's representatives to the world. Some days this duty may seem overwhelming, but remember—Christ is the One who will keep us "blameless unto the coming of our Lord Jesus Christ" (1 Thessalonians 5:23).

Who shall also confirm you unto the end, that ye may be blameless in the day of our Lord Jesus Christ.   *1 Corinthians 1:8*

That ye may be blameless and harmless, the sons of God, without rebuke, in the midst of a crooked and perverse nation, among whom ye shine as lights in the world.
Philippians 2:15

Keep back thy servant also from presumptuous sins; let them not have dominion over me: then shall I be innocent from the great transgression.   *Psalm 19:13*

And they were both righteous before God, walking in all the commandments and ordinances of the Lord blameless.   *Luke 1:6*

Pure religion and undefiled before God and the Father is this, To visit the fatherless and widows in their affliction, and to keep himself unspotted from the world. *James 1:27*

I will wash mine hands in innocency: so will I compass thine altar, O Lord. *Psalm 26:6*

And in their mouth was found no guile: for they are without fault before the throne of God. *Revelation 14:5*

And the very God of peace sanctify you wholly; and I pray God your whole spirit and soul and body be preserved blameless unto the coming of our Lord Jesus Christ.
1 Thessalonians 5:23

Blessed is the man unto whom the Lord imputeth not iniquity, and in whose spirit there is no guile. *Psalm 32:2*

Wherefore laying aside all malice, and all guile, and hypocrisies, and envies, and all evil speakings,

As newborn babes, desire the sincere milk of the word, that ye may grow thereby:

If so be ye have tasted that the Lord is gracious. *1 Peter 2:1–3*

BODY OF CHRIST

As single people, we never need to feel as though we are loners or outsiders, for we belong to a vital and living group, a spiritual family: Christ's own Body, the Church. Each one of us is needed and important, with our own role to fill in the workings of His Body.

Endeavouring to keep the unity of the Spirit in the bond of peace.

There is one body, and one Spirit, even as ye are called in one hope of your calling.
Ephesians 4:3–4

And he gave some, apostles; and some, prophets; and some, evangelists; and some, pastors and teachers;

For the perfecting of the saints, for the work of the ministry, for the edifying of the body of Christ. *Ephesians 4:11–12*

For as we have many members in one body, and all members have not the same office:

So we, being many, are one body in Christ, and every one members one of another. *Romans 12:4–5*

And let us consider one another to provoke unto love and to good works:

Not forsaking the assembling of ourselves together. . .but exhorting one another: and so much the more, as ye see the day approaching. *Hebrews 10:24–25*

For by one Spirit are we all baptized into one body, whether we be Jews or Gentiles, whether we be bond or free; and have been all made to drink into one Spirit.

For the body is not one member, but many.

If the foot shall say, Because I am not the hand, I am not of the body; is it therefore not of the body?

And if the ear shall say, Because I am not the eye, I am not of the body; is it therefore not of the body?

If the whole body were an eye, where were the hearing? If the whole were hearing, where were the smelling?

But now hath God set the members every one of them in the body, as it hath pleased him.

And if they were all one member, where were the body?

But now are they many members, yet but one body.

And the eye cannot say unto the hand, I have no need of thee: nor again the head to the feet, I have no need of you.

Nay, much more those members of the body, which seem to be more feeble, are necessary:

. . .but God hath tempered the body together, having given more abundant honour to that part which lacked:

That there should be no schism in the

body; but that the members should have the same care one for another.

And whether one member suffer, all the members suffer with it; or one member be honoured, all the members rejoice with it.

Now ye are the body of Christ. . .
1 Corinthians 12:13–22, 24–27

For we being many are one bread, and one body: for we are all partakers of that one bread. *1 Corinthians 10:17*

Now therefore ye are no more strangers and foreigners, but fellowcitizens with the saints, and of the household of God.
Ephesians 2:19

CHARITABLE

The charity that the Bible speaks of is an active love for those around us. Our world puts a great deal of emphasis on our emotions, but charity has less to do with how we feel than it does with how we act. Charity means behaving lovingly even if we're having a bad day; it means putting the needs of others ahead of our own. Most of all it means letting Christ use our hands and feet and mouths, so that His love will become real to the world around us.

And though I have the gift of prophecy, and understand all mysteries, and all knowledge; and though I have all faith, so that I could remove mountains, and have not charity, I am nothing.

And though I bestow all my goods to feed the poor, and though I give my body to be burned, and have not charity, it profiteth me nothing.   *1 Corinthians 13:2–3*

Though I speak with the tongues of men and of angels, and have not charity, I am become as sounding brass, or a tinkling cymbal.
1 Corinthians 13:1

Charity never faileth: but whether there be prophecies, they shall fail; whether there be tongues, they shall cease; whether there be knowledge, it shall vanish away.
1 Corinthians 13:8

And above all things have fervent charity among yourselves: for charity shall cover the multitude of sins.   *1 Peter 4:8*

Beloved, thou doest faithfully whatsoever thou doest to the brethren, and to strangers;
    Which have borne witness of thy charity before the church.   *3 John 1:5–6*

Be kindly affectioned one to another with brotherly love; in honor preferring one another.   *Romans 12:10*

Charity suffereth long, and is kind; charity envieth not; charity vaunteth not itself, is not puffed up,
    Doth not behave itself unseemly, seeketh not her own, is not easily provoked, thinketh no evil;
    Rejoiceth not in iniquity, but rejoiceth in the truth;
    Beareth all things, believeth all things, hopeth all things, endureth all things.
    1 Corinthians 13:4–7

Whosoever believeth that Jesus is the Christ is born of God: and every one that loveth him that begat loveth him also that is begotten of him.   *1 John 5:1*

Owe no man any thing, but to love one another: for he that loveth another hath fulfilled the law.   *Romans 13:8*

And to godliness brotherly kindness; and to brotherly kindness charity.

For if these things be in you, and abound, they make you that ye shall neither be barren nor unfruitful in the knowledge of our Lord Jesus Christ.   *2 Peter 1:7–8*

But as touching brotherly love ye need not that I write unto you: for ye yourselves are taught of God to love one another.
1 Thessalonians 4:9

Beloved, let us love one another: for love is of God; and every one that loveth is born of God, and knoweth God.

He that loveth not knoweth not God; for God is love.   *1 John 4:7–8*

Seeing ye have purified your souls in obeying the truth through the Spirit unto unfeigned love of the brethren, see that ye love one another with a pure heart fervently.
1 Peter 1:22

CHRISTLIKE

As single people, we have many goals that are important to us. We want to achieve a certain degree of education or we aim for a specific job or salary or relationship. Earthly goals are fine—so long as we do not forget that our ultimate goal is to be like Christ.

I am crucified with Christ: nevertheless I live; yet not I, but Christ liveth in me: and the life which I now live in the flesh I live by the faith of the Son of God, who loved me, and gave himself for me.

Galatians 2:20

Therefore if any man be in Christ, he is a new creature: old things are passed away; behold, all things are become new.

2 Corinthians 5:17

Blessed be the God and Father of our Lord Jesus Christ, who hath blessed us with all spiritual blessings in heavenly places in Christ.   *Ephesians 1:3*

Now thanks be unto God, which always causeth us to triumph in Christ, and maketh manifest the savour of his knowledge by us in every place.

For we are unto God a sweet savour of Christ, in them that are saved, and in them that perish.   *2 Corinthians 2:14–15*

Be ye followers of me, even as I also am of Christ.   *1 Corinthians 11:1*

For who hath known the mind of the Lord, that he may instruct him? But we have the mind of Christ.   *1 Corinthians 2:16*

Know ye not, that so many of us as were baptized into Jesus Christ were baptized into his death?

Therefore we are buried with him by baptism into death: that like as Christ was raised up from the dead by the glory of the Father, even so we also should walk in newness of life.

For if we have been planted together in the likeness of his death, we shall be also in the likeness of his resurrection:

Knowing this, that our old man is crucified with him, that the body of sin might be destroyed, that henceforth we should not serve sin. . . .

Now if we be dead with Christ, we believe that we shall also live with him:

Knowing that Christ being raised from the dead dieth no more; death hath no more dominion over him.

For in that he died, he died unto sin once: but in that he liveth, he liveth unto God.

Likewise reckon ye also yourselves to be dead indeed unto sin, but alive unto God through Jesus Christ our Lord.

Romans 6:3–6, 8–11

COMFORT

At the end of a hard day, we all need someone who will understand and comfort us. Even if we are alone in the world, we still have Someone who will care for and comfort us when we are troubled.

In the multitude of my thoughts within me thy comforts delight my soul.

Psalm 94:19

Blessed be God, even the Father of our Lord Jesus Christ, the Father of mercies, and the God of all comfort;

Who comforteth us in all our tribulation, that we may be able to comfort them which are in any trouble, by the comfort wherewith we ourselves are comforted of God.

2 Corinthians 1:3–4

Sing, O heavens; and be joyful, O earth; and break forth into singing, O mountains: for the LORD hath comforted his people, and will have mercy upon his afflicted.

Isaiah 49:13

As ye know how we exhorted and comforted and charged every one of you, as a father doth his children,

That ye would walk worthy of God, who hath called you unto his kingdom and glory.

1 Thessalonians 2:11–12

And I will pray the Father, and he shall give you another Comforter, that he may abide with you for ever. *John 14:16*

That their hearts might be comforted, being knit together in love, and unto all riches of the full assurance of understanding, to the acknowledgement of the mystery of God, and of the Father, and of Christ.

Colossians 2:2

But when the Comforter is come, whom I will send unto you from the Father, even the Spirit of truth, which proceedeth from the Father, he shall testify of me. *John 15:26*

Like as a father pitieth his children, so the LORD pitieth them that fear him.

For he knoweth our frame; he remembereth that we are dust. *Psalm 103:13–14*

Yea, though I walk through the valley of the shadow of death, I will fear no evil: for thou art with me; thy rod and thy staff they comfort me. *Psalm 23:4*

For the LORD shall comfort Zion: he will comfort all her waste places; and he will make her wilderness like Eden, and her desert like the garden of the LORD; joy and gladness shall be found therein, thanksgiving, and the voice of melody. *Isaiah 51:3*

Thou, which hast shewed me great and sore troubles, shalt quicken me again, and shalt bring me up again from the depths of the earth.

Thou shalt increase my greatness, and comfort me on every side.

Psalm 71:20–21

He brought me to the banqueting house, and his banner over me was love.

Stay me with flagons, comfort me with apples. . . *Song of Solomon 2:4–5*

Therefore the redeemed of the LORD shall return, and come with singing unto Zion; and everlasting joy shall be upon their head: they shall obtain gladness and joy; and sorrow and mourning shall flee away.

I, even I, am he that comforteth you. . . *Isaiah 51:11–12*

Now our Lord Jesus Christ himself, and God, even our Father, which hath loved us, and hath given us everlasting consolation and good hope through grace,

Comfort your hearts, and stablish you in every good word and work.

2 Thessalonians 2:16–17

CONSCIENTIOUS

Sometimes we'd like to be lazy, cut a few corners, take the easy way. But God calls us to be conscientious about whatever we do, remembering that we represent Him to the world.

And herein do I exercise myself, to have always a conscience void of offence toward God, and toward men.   *Acts 24:16*

Now the end of the commandment is charity out of a pure heart, and of a good conscience, and of faith unfeigned.   *1 Timothy 1:5*

Dearly beloved, I beseech you as strangers and pilgrims, abstain from fleshly lusts, which war against the soul;

Having your conversation honest among the Gentiles: that, whereas they speak against you as evildoers, they may by your good works, which they shall behold, glorify God in the day of visitation.
                                                1 Peter 2:11–12

But that on the good ground are they, which in an honest and good heart, having heard the word, keep it, and bring forth fruit with patience.   *Luke 8:15*

Holding the mystery of the faith in a pure conscience.   *1 Timothy 3:9*

Holding faith, and a good conscience; which some having put away concerning faith have made shipwreck.   *1 Timothy 1:19*

Finally, brethren, whatsoever things are true, whatsoever things are honest, whatsoever things are just, whatsoever things are pure, whatsoever things are lovely, whatsoever things are of good report; if there be any virtue, and if there be any praise, think on these things.   *Philippians 4:8*

Providing for honest things, not only in the sight of the Lord, but also in the sight of men.   *2 Corinthians 8:21*

Let us hold fast the profession of our faith without wavering; (for he is faithful that promised).   *Hebrews 10:23*

COURAGE

Sometimes the world can seem like a frightening place. No matter what we face, though, we do not have to be scared or nervous. Over and over again, the Bible repeats the same command: Be not afraid, fear not. God goes with us wherever we go, and He is greater than anything we face in the world.

Be strong and of a good courage. . .

Only be thou strong and very courageous, that thou mayest observe to do according to all the law, which Moses my servant commanded thee: turn not from it to the right hand or to the left, that thou mayest prosper whithersoever thou goest.

Joshua 1:6–7

Why art thou cast down, O my soul? and why art thou disquieted within me? hope in God: for I shall yet praise him, who is the health of my countenance, and my God.

Psalm 43:5

Yea, though I walk through the valley of the shadow of death, I will fear no evil: for thou art with me; thy rod and thy staff they comfort me. *Psalm 23:4*

But straightway Jesus spake unto them, saying, "Be of good cheer; it is I; be not afraid."

Matthew 14:27

Fear not, little flock, for it is your Father's good pleasure to give you the kingdom.

Luke 12:32

Fear thou not; for I am with thee: be not dismayed; for I am thy God: I will strengthen thee; yea, I will help thee; yea, I will uphold thee with the right hand of my righteousness.

Isaiah 41:10

But whoso hearkeneth unto me shall dwell safely, and shall be quiet from fear of evil

Proverbs 1:33

. . .Be content with such things as ye have: for he hath said, I will never leave thee, nor forsake thee.

So that we may boldly say, The Lord is my helper, I will not fear what man shall do unto me.

Hebrews 13:5–6

He shall cover thee with his feathers, and under his wings shalt thou trust: his truth shall be thy shield and buckler.

Thou shalt not be afraid for the terror by night; nor for the arrow that flieth by day;

Nor for the pestilence that walketh in darkness; nor for the destruction that wasteth at noonday. . . .

For he shall give his angels charge over thee, to keep thee in all thy ways.

Psalm 91:4–6, 11

For God hath not given us the spirit of fear; but of power, and of love, and of a sound mind. *2 Timothy 1:7*

Peace I leave with you, my peace I give unto you: not as the world giveth, give I unto you. Let not your heart be troubled, neither let it be afraid. *John 14:27*

Be not afraid of sudden fear, neither of the desolation of the wicked, when it cometh.

For the LORD shall be thy confidence, and shall keep thy foot from being taken.
Proverbs 3:25–26

For ye have not received the spirit of bondage again to fear; but ye have received the Spirit of adoption, whereby we cry, Abba, Father. *Romans 8:15*

DEPRESSION

All of us get depressed sometimes. When we do, we need to give our sadness to the Lord, knowing that only He has the power to comfort us.

He that goeth forth and weepeth, bearing precious seed, shall doubtless come again with rejoicing, bringing his sheaves with him. *Psalm 126:6*

Why art thou cast down, O my soul? and why art thou disquieted in me? hope thou in God. . . *Psalm 42:5*

He shall call upon me, and I will answer him: I will be with him in trouble. . .
Psalm 91:15

Be careful for nothing; but in every thing by prayer and supplication with thanksgiving let your requests be made known unto God.
And the peace of God, which passeth all understanding, shall keep your hearts and minds through Christ Jesus.
Philippians 4:6–7

Surely he hath borne our griefs, and carried our sorrows. . . *Isaiah 53:4*

. . .He hath sent me to bind up the broken-hearted. . . *Isaiah 61:1*

. . .I have called thee by thy name; thou at mine.

When thou passest through the waters, I will be with thee: and through the rivers, they shall not overflow thee. . .

Isaiah 43:1–2

I, even I, am he that comforteth you.

Isaiah 51:12

. . .The Father of mercies, and the God of all comfort;

Who comforteth us in all our tribulation, that we may be able to comfort them which are in any trouble, by the comfort wherewith we ourselves are comforted of God.

For as the sufferings of Christ abound in us, so our consolation also aboundeth by Christ.   *2 Corinthians 1:3–5*

Cast thy burden upon the LORD, and he shall sustain thee. . .   *Psalm 55:22*

As one whom his mother comforteth, so will I comfort you. . .   *Isaiah 66:13*

DISAPPOINTMENT

We all have hopes that end up being disappointed. Whether we long for a particular job —or a relationship with a particular someone—sometimes we don't get the thing we long for. Disappointment hurts, but we can depend on God to carry us through it.

Behold, I have refined thee, but not with silver; I have chosen thee in the furnace of affliction. *Isaiah 48:10*

. . .We must through much tribulation enter into the kingdom of God. *Acts 14:22*

Although the fig tree shall not blossom, neither shall fruit be in the vines: the labour of the olive shall fail, and the fields shall yield no meat; the flock shall be cut off from the fold, and there shall be no herd in the stalls:
    Yet I will rejoice in the LORD, I will joy in the God of my salvation.

Habbakuk 3:17–18

I have learned, in whatsoever state I am, . . . to be content. *Philippians 4:11*

All men forsook me. . .
    Notwithstanding the Lord stood with me, and strengthened me. . .

2 Timothy 4:16–17

. . .He faileth not. . . *Zephaniah 3:5*

. . .The LORD God of thy fathers hath said unto thee; fear not, neither be discouraged.

Deuteronomy 1:21

A bruised reed shall he not break. . .

Isaiah 42:3

When the poor and needy seek water, and there is none, and their tongue faileth for thirst, I the LORD will hear them, I the God of Israel will not forsake them.

I will open rivers in high places, and fountains in the midst of the valleys: I will make the wilderness a pool of water, and the dry land springs of water.

Isaiah 41:17–18

Then I said, I have laboured in vain, I have spent my strength for nought, and in vain: yet surely my judgment is with the LORD, and my work with my God.

And now, saith the LORD that formed me from the womb to be his servant. . .yet shall I be glorious in the eyes of the LORD, and my God shall be my strength.

Isaiah 49:4–5

Thus saith the LORD; Refrain thy voice from weeping, and thine eyes from tears: for thy work shall be rewarded. . . *Jeremiah 31:16*

DISCERNMENT

Sometimes it's hard to see what we should do. The world offers so many choices—how can we decide which are the best options for us to choose? When we feel confused about which path to take, then we need to ask God to give us the gift of discernment, so that we can clearly see what He wants us to do.

Whoso keepeth the commandment shall feel no evil thing: and a wise man's heart discerneth both time and judgment.

Ecclesiastes 8:5

. . .Cause me to know the way wherein I should walk; for I lift up my soul unto thee.

Psalm 143:8

But the natural man receiveth not the things of the Spirit of God: for they are foolishness unto him: neither can he know them, because they are spiritually discerned.

1 Corinthians 2:14

Then shall ye return, and discern between the righteous and the wicked, between him that serveth God and him that serveth him not.

Malachi 3:18

The LORD is my shepherd. . .

. . .He leadeth me in the paths of righteousness for his name's sake.

Psalm 23:1, 3

Give therefore thy servant an understanding heart to judge thy people, that I may discern between good and bad; for who is able to judge this thy so great a people?

And the speech pleased the Lord, that Solomon had asked this thing.

And God said unto him, "Because thou hast asked this thing, and hast not asked for thyself long life; neither hast asked riches for thyself, nor hast asked the life of thine enemies; but hast asked for thyself understanding to discern judgment;

Behold, I have done according to thy words. . ." *1 Kings 3:9–12*

And thine ears shall hear a word behind thee, saying, This is the way, walk ye in it, when ye turn to the right hand, and when ye turn to the left. *Isaiah 30:21*

DISCRETION

Someone who is discreet uses good judgment in the way he or she lives. As Christ's representatives, this is a quality we need to cultivate, so that we do not give Christianity a bad name.

My son, let not them depart from thine eyes: keep sound wisdom and discretion:

So shall they be life unto thy soul, and grace to thy neck.   *Proverbs 3:21–22*

A good man sheweth favour, and lendeth: he will guide his affairs with discretion.
                                                    Psalm 112:5

My son, attend unto my wisdom, and bow thine ear to my understanding:

That thou mayest regard discretion, and that thy lips may keep knowledge.
                                                    Proverbs 5:1–2

When wisdom entereth into thine heart, and knowledge is pleasant unto thy soul;

Discretion shall preserve thee, understanding shall keep thee:

To deliver thee from the evil man, from the man that speaketh froward things.
                                                    Proverbs 2:10–12

For his God doth instruct him to discretion, and doth teach him.   *Isaiah 28:26*

And when Jesus saw that he answered discreetly, he said unto him, "Thou art not far from the kingdom of God. . . ."

Mark 12:34

To give subtilty to the simple, to the young man knowledge and discretion.

Proverbs 1:4

As a jewel of gold in a swine's snout, so is a fair woman which is without discretion.

Proverbs 11:22

The discretion of a man deferreth his anger; and it is his glory to pass over a transgression.

Proverbs 19:11

. . .Hold fast that which is good.

Abstain from all appearance of evil.

And the very God of peace sanctify you wholly; and I pray God whole spirit and soul and body be preserved blameless unto the coming of our Lord Jesus Christ.

1 Thessalonians 5:21–23

DUTIFULNESS

As Christ's followers, most of us want to do our duty—but sometimes we're not sure just what our duty is. The Bible makes very clear, though, just what our duty is.

Let us hear the conclusion of the whole matter: Fear God, and keep his commandments: for this is the whole duty of man.

Ecclesiastes 12:13

Will the LORD be pleased with thousands of rams, or with ten thousands of rivers of oil? shall I give my firstborn for my transgression, the fruit of my body for the sin of my soul?

He hath shewed thee, O man, what is good; and what doth the LORD require of thee, but to do justly, and to love mercy, and to walk humbly with thy God?

Micah 6:7–8

Moreover it is required in stewards, that a man be found faithful.

1 Corinthians 4:2

And, behold, one came and said unto him, "Good Master, what good thing shall I do, that I may have eternal life?"

And he said unto him. . . "if thou wilt enter into life, keep the commandments."

Matthew 19:16–17

And now, Israel, what doth the LORD thy God require of thee, but to fear the LORD thy God, to walk in all his ways, and to love him, and to serve the LORD thy God with all thy heart and with all thy soul,

To keep the commandments of the LORD, and his statutes, which I command thee this day for thy good? *Deuteronomy 10:12–13*

O that there were such an heart in them, that they would fear me, and keep all my commandments always, that it might be well with them, and with their children for ever!
Deuteronomy 5:29

A new commandment I give unto you, That ye love one another; as I have loved you, that ye also love one another.

By this shall all men know that ye are my disciples, if ye have love one to another.
John 13:34–35

And hereby we do know that we know him, if we keep his commandments.

He that saith, I know him, and keepeth not his commandments, is a liar, and the truth is not in him.

But whoso keepeth his word, in him verily is the love of God perfected: hereby know we that we are in him.

He that saith he abideth in him ought himself also so to walk, even as he walked.
1 John 2:3–6

And whatsoever we ask, we receive of him, because we keep his commandments, and do those things that are pleasing in his sight.

1 John 3:22

I made haste, and delayed not to keep thy commandments.   *Psalm 119:60*

Ye shall walk in all the ways which the LORD your God hath commanded you, that ye may live, and that it may be well with you, and that ye may prolong your days in the land which ye shall possess.

Deuteronomy 5:33

EARNESTNESS

Sometimes we take our Christianity for granted. We shuffle along, not really paying attention, our minds fixed on other things. The dictionary says, though, that if we do something earnestly then we do it seriously, with concentration and effort. We need to live our lives for Christ with earnestness, rather than with carelessness, putting our whole effort into our spiritual walk.

But covet earnestly the best gifts: and yet shew I unto you a more excellent way.

1 Corinthians 12:31

Therefore we ought to give the more earnest heed to the things which we have heard, lest at any time we should let them slip.

For if the word spoken by angels was stedfast, and every transgression and disobedience received a just recompence of reward;

How shall we escape, if we neglect so great salvation. . .   *Hebrews 2:1–3*

Seeing ye have purified your souls in obeying the truth through the Spirit unto unfeigned love of the brethren, see that ye love one another with a pure heart fervently.

1 Peter 1:22

Be. . .fervent in spirit; serving the Lord.

Romans 12:10–11

. . .The effectual fervent prayer of a righteous man availeth much.   *James 5:16*

According to my earnest expectation and my hope, that in nothing I shall be ashamed, but that with all boldness, as always, so now also Christ shall be magnified in my body, whether it be by life, or by death.

For to me to live is Christ, and to die is gain.   *Philippians 1:20–21*

. . .It was needful for me to write unto you, and exhort you that ye should earnestly contend for the faith which was once delivered unto the saints.   *Jude 3*

EDIFYING

Something that is edifying instructs and improves us spiritually. Much of what we find in the world, whether it's television or music or merely conversations, is destructive to our spirituality, rather than edifying. As Christians, our responsibility is to see that as much as possible we take in material that is edifying. We need to see that what comes out of us in our conversations is also edifying,

For God hath not appointed us to wrath, but to obtain salvation by our Lord Jesus Christ. . .

Wherefore comfort yourselves together, and edify one another, even as also ye do.
1 Thessalonians 5:9, 11

Let no corrupt communication proceed out of your mouth, but that which is good to the use of edifying, that it may minister grace unto the hearers.   *Ephesians 4:29*

Neither give heed to fables and endless genealogies, which minister questions, rather than godly edifying which is in faith: so do.
1 Timothy 1:4

All things are lawful for me, but all things are not expedient: all things are lawful for me, but all things edify not.
1 Corinthians 10:23

And he gave some, apostles; and some, prophets; and some, evangelists; and some, pastors and teachers;

For the perfecting of the saints, for the work of the ministry, for the edifying of the body of Christ. *Ephesians 4:11–12*

. . .Knowledge puffeth up, but charity edifieth. *1 Corinthians 8:1*

From whom the whole body fitly joined together and compacted by that which every joint supplieth, according to the effectual working in the measure of every part, maketh increase of the body unto the edifying of itself in love. *Ephesians 4:16*

Let us therefore follow after the things which make for peace, and things wherewith one may edify another. *Romans 14:19*

FAITHFUL

Many times we are disappointed by our human relationships. How good it is to know that no matter how many times people hurt us, God will always be faithful to us.

Know therefore that the LORD thy God, he is God, the faithful God, which keepeth covenant and mercy with them that love him and keep his commandments to a thousand generations. *Deuteronomy 7:9*

Thy mercy, O LORD, is in the heavens; and thy faithfulness reacheth unto the clouds.
Psalm 36:5

O LORD, thou art my God; I will exalt thee, I will praise thy name; for thou hast done wonderful things; thy counsels of old are faithfulness and truth. *Isaiah 25:1*

Let us hold fast the profession of our faith without wavering; (for he is faithful that promised). *Hebrews 10:23*

Thus saith the LORD. . .because of the LORD that is faithful, and the Holy One of Israel, and he shall choose thee.
　　Thus saith the LORD, In an acceptable time have I heard thee, and in a day of salvation have I helped thee: and I will preserve thee. . . *Isaiah 49:7–8*

If we confess our sins, he is faithful and just to forgive us our sins, and to cleanse us from all unrighteousness. *1 John 1:9*

All thy commandments are faithful. . .

For ever, O LORD, thy word is settled in heaven.

Thy faithfulness is unto all generations: thou hast established the earth, and it abideth.
Psalm 119:86, 89–90

Thy testimonies that thou hast commanded are righteous and very faithful.
Psalm 119:138

This I recall to my mind, therefore have I hope.

It is of the LORD's mercies that we are not consumed, because his compassions fail not.

They are new every morning: great is thy faithfulness.

The LORD is my portion, saith my soul; therefore will I hope in him.

The LORD is good unto them that wait for him, to the soul that seeketh him.
Lamentations 3:21–25

Through faith also Sara herself received strength to conceive seed, and was delivered of a child when she was past age, because she judged him faithful who had promised.
Hebrews 11:11

Faithful is he that calleth you, who also will do it. *1 Thessalonians 5:24*

God is faithful, by whom ye were called unto the fellowship of his Son Jesus Christ our Lord. *1 Corinthians 1:9*

. . .God is faithful, who will not suffer you to be tempted above that ye are able. . .
1 Corinthians 10:13

I will sing of the mercies of the LORD for ever: with my mouth will I make known thy faithfulness to all generations.

For I have said, Mercy shall be built up for ever: thy faithfulness shalt thou establish in the very heavens. . . .

And the heavens shall praise thy wonders, O LORD: thy faithfulness also in the congregation of the saints. . . .

But my faithfulness and my mercy shall be with him: and in my name shall his horn be exalted.

. . .He shall cry unto me, Thou art my father, my God, and the rock of my salvation.

. . .My mercy will I keep for him for evermore, and my covenant shall stand fast with him.

. . .Blessed be the LORD for evermore. Amen, and Amen.

Psalm 89: 1–2, 5, 24, 26, 28, 52

FORGIVENESS

No matter how many mistakes we make, God's forgiveness is never used up. Since we have been forgiven by God for so much, we need to forgive others, no matter how many times they hurt us.

If my people, which are called by my name, shall humble themselves, and pray, and seek my face, and turn from their wicked ways; then will I hear from heaven, and will forgive their sin, and will heal their land.

2 Chronicles 7:14

. . .Lord, how oft shall my brother sin against me, and I forgive him? till seven times?

Jesus saith unto him, "I say not unto thee, Until seven times: but, Until seventy times seven." *Matthew 18:21–22*

. . .And the Lord shall raise him up; and if he have committed sins, they shall be forgiven him. *James 5:15*

For thou, Lord, art good, and ready to forgive; and plenteous in mercy unto all them that call upon thee. *Psalm 86:5*

Wherefore I say unto thee, Her sins, which are many, are forgiven; for she loved much: but to whom little is forgiven, the same loveth little. *Luke 7:47*

Bless the LORD, O my soul, and forget not all his benefits:

Who forgiveth all thine iniquities; who healeth all thy diseases;

Who redeemeth thy life from destruction; who crowneth thee with lovingkindness and tender mercies.   *Psalm 103:2–4*

Look upon mine affliction and my pain; and forgive all my sins.   *Psalm 25:18*

Blessed is he whose transgression is forgiven, whose sin is covered.   *Psalm 32:1*

And when ye stand praying, forgive, if ye have ought against any: that your Father also which is in heaven may forgive you your trespasses.

But if ye do not forgive, neither will your Father which is in heaven forgive your trespasses.   *Mark 11:25–26*

And be ye kind one to another, tenderhearted, forgiving one another, even as God for Christ's sake hath forgiven you.

Ephesians 4:32

Judge not, and ye shall not be judged: condemn not, and ye shall not be condemned: forgive, and ye shall be forgiven.

Luke 6:37

FRUITFULNESS

Sometimes we feel we have to be productive in the ways that our culture accepts. We have to have a certain type of job, earn a certain salary, get married and have children by a certain age, or we feel we have failed. The Bible reminds us, though, that there are other ways to be productive than merely the ones our culture recognizes. True fruitfulness springs from our relationship with God, and only as we are joined with Him can we be truly productive.

But his delight is in the law of the LORD; and in his law doth he meditate day and night.

And he shall be like a tree planted by the rivers of water, that bringeth forth his fruit in his season; his leaf also shall not wither; and whatsoever he doeth shall prosper.

Psalm 1:2–3

For if these things be in you, and abound, they make you that ye shall neither be barren nor unfruitful in the knowledge of our Lord Jesus Christ.   *2 Peter 1:8*

I am the true vine, and my Father is the husbandman.

Every branch in me that beareth not fruit he taketh away: and every branch that beareth fruit, he purgeth it, that it may bring forth more fruit.   *John 15:1–2*

I will be as the dew unto Israel: he shall grow as the lily, and cast forth his roots as Lebanon. *Hosea 14:5*

But the fruit of the Spirit is love, joy, peace, longsuffering, gentleness, goodness, faith,

Meekness, temperance: against such there is no law. *Galatians 5:22–23*

That ye might walk worthy of the Lord unto all pleasing, being fruitful in every good work, and increasing in the knowledge of God. *Colossians 1:10*

And the LORD shall guide thee continually, and satisfy thy soul in drought, and make fat thy bones: and thou shalt be like a watered garden, and like a spring of water, whose waters fail not. *Isaiah 58:11*

If ye walk in my statutes, and keep my commandments, and do them. . .

I will have respect unto you, and make you fruitful, and multiply you, and establish my covenant with you. *Leviticus 26:3, 9*

GIFTED

We're not children any longer—but we still like to receive presents. The best gifts of all, though, come from our heavenly Father.

If ye then, being evil, know how to give good gifts unto your children, how much more shall your Father which is in heaven give good things to them that ask him?
Matthew 7:11

For by grace are ye saved through faith; and that not of yourselves: it is the gift of God:
Not of works, lest any man should boast.
Ephesians 2:8–9

Now there are diversities of gifts, but the same Spirit.
And there are differences of administrations, but the same Lord.
And there are diversities of operations, but it is the same God which worketh all in all.
But the manifestation of the Spirit is given to every man to profit withal.
1 Corinthians 12:4–7

But unto every one of us is given grace according to the measure of the gift of Christ.
Wherefore he saith, When he ascended up on high, he led captivity captive, and gave gifts unto men. *Ephesians 4:7–8*

Every good gift and every perfect gift is from above, and cometh down from the Father of lights, with whom is no variableness, neither shadow of turning.   *James 1:17*

Having then gifts differing according to the grace that is given to us. . .   *Romans 12:6*

For the wages of sin is death; but the gift of God is eternal life through Jesus Christ our Lord.   *Romans 6:23*

For the gifts and calling of God are without repentance.   *Romans 11:29*

GRACE

In a world where we have to work so hard for every degree and advancement and salary raise, God's grace is one thing we need do nothing to earn. Instead, it is His gift to us through Jesus, and though we are undeserving, day by day He pours His grace down on us freely.

For the LORD God is a sun and shield: the LORD will give grace and glory: no good thing will he withhold from them that walk uprightly.   *Psalm 84:11*

My son, hear the instruction of thy father, and forsake not the law of thy mother:
    For they shall be an ornament of grace unto thy head, and chains about thy neck.
                    Proverbs 1:8–9

And therefore will the LORD wait, that he may be gracious unto you, and therefore will he be exalted, that he may have mercy upon you: for the LORD is a God of judgment: blessed are all they that wait for him.
                    Isaiah 30:18

The LORD bless thee, and keep thee:
    The LORD make his face shine upon thee, and be gracious unto thee:
    The LORD lift up his countenance upon thee, and give thee peace.
                    Numbers 6:24–26

As newborn babes, desire the sincere milk of the word, that ye may grow thereby:

If so be ye have tasted that the Lord is gracious. *1 Peter 2:2–3*

And the Word was made flesh, and dwelt among us, (and we beheld his glory, the glory as of the only begotten of the Father,) full of grace and truth. *John 1:14*

But thou, O Lord, art a God full of compassion, and gracious, longsuffering, and plenteous in mercy and truth. *Psalm 86:15*

But grow in grace, and in the knowledge of our Lord and Saviour Jesus Christ. . . .

2 Peter 3:18

HONORABLE

When we honor someone, we respect them. We listen to what they have to say. We treat them with consideration. The world tends to honor only those who have some type of power—but the Bible has other ideas. Among others, we are to honor our parents; although we are adults now, God asks us to listen to our parents with respect and treat them with consideration.

If any man serve me, let him follow me; and where I am, there shall also my servant be: if any man serve me, him will my Father honour. *John 12:26*

Honour thy father and mother; (which is the first commandment with promise;)

That it may be well with thee, and thou mayest live long on the earth.

Ephesians 6:2–3

. . .All men should honour the Son, even as thy honour the Father. He that honoureth not the Son honoureth not the Father which hath sent him. *John 5:23*

Happy is the man that findeth wisdom, and the man that getteth understanding. . . .

Length of days is in her right hand; and in her left hand riches and honour.

Proverbs 3:13, 16

Honour thy father and thy mother: that thy days may be long upon the land which the LORD thy God giveth thee. *Exodus 20:12*

Honour the LORD with thy substance, and with the firstfruits of all thine increase.
Proverbs 3:9

Be kindly affectioned one to another with brotherly love; in honour preferring one another. *Romans 12:10*

For this is the will of God, even your sanctification. . .

That every one of you should know how to possess his vessel in sanctification and honour. *1 Thessalonians 4:3–4*

HOPE

The world tends to have a negative outlook on life, but as Christians we have something the world lacks: hope. Hope is more than feeling cheery and optimistic. Instead, it is the strong, practical belief in God's salvation, no matter what our present circumstances. It is like a bridge that carries us confidently across whatever troubles the present holds.

But let us, who are of the day, be sober, putting on the breastplate of faith and love; and for an helmet, the hope of salvation.

1 Thessalonians 5:8

Beloved, now are we the sons of God, and it doth not yet appear what we shall be: but we know that, when he shall appear, we shall be like him; for we shall see him as he is.

And every man that hath this hope in him purifieth himself, even as he is pure.

1 John 3:2–3

Blessed be the God and Father of our Lord Jesus Christ, which according to his abundant mercy hath begotten us again unto a lively hope by the resurrection of Jesus Christ from the dead. *1 Peter 1:3*

Blessed is the man that trusteth in the LORD, and whose hope the LORD is.

Jeremiah 17:7

. . .We glory in tribulations also: knowing that tribulation worketh patience;

And patience, experience; and experience, hope:

And hope maketh not ashamed; because the love of God is shed abroad in our hearts by the Holy Ghost which is given unto us.
Romans 5:3–5

The hope of the righteous shall be gladness: but the expectation of the wicked shall perish. *Proverbs 10:28*

And we desire that every one of you do shew the same diligence to the full assurance of hope unto the end. *Hebrews 6:11*

Now the God of hope fill you with all joy and peace in believing, that ye may abound in hope, through the power of the Holy Ghost. *Romans 15:13*

Teaching us that, denying ungodliness and worldly lusts, we should live soberly, righteously, and godly, in this present world;

Looking for that blessed hope, and the glorious appearing of the great God and our Saviour Jesus Christ. *Titus 2:12–13*

But I would not have you to be ignorant, brethren, concerning them which are asleep, that ye sorrow not, even as others which have no hope. *1 Thessalonians 4:13*

That by two immutable things, in which it was impossible for God to lie, we might have a strong consolation, who have fled for refuge to lay hold upon the hope set before us:

Which hope we have as an anchor of the soul, both sure and stedfast, and which entereth into that within the veil.

Hebrews 6:18–19

Why art thou cast down, O my soul? and why art thou disquieted in me? hope thou in God: for I shall yet praise him for the help of his countenance. *Psalm 42:5*

For I know the thoughts that I think toward you, saith the LORD, thoughts of peace, and not of evil, to give you an expected end.

Jeremiah 29:11

For whatsoever things were written aforetime were written for our learning, that we through patience and comfort of the scriptures might have hope. *Romans 15:4*

HUMILITY

Sometimes we value ourselves too highly. We are infinitely precious in God's eyes, but we need to remember that our value comes not from our own efforts, but instead springs from God's unmerited grace.

When men are cast down, then thou shalt say, There is lifting up; and he shall save the humble person. *Job 22:29*

But he giveth more grace. Wherefore he saith, God resisteth the proud, but giveth grace unto the humble. *James 4:6*

Whosoever therefore shall humble himself as this little child, the same is greatest in the kingdom of heaven. *Matthew 18:4*

. . .Yea, all of you be subject to one another, and be clothed with humility: for God resisteth the proud, and giveth grace to the humble.
    Humble yourselves therefore under the mighty hand of God. . .
    Casting all your care upon him; for he careth for you. *1 Peter 5:5–7*

Surely he scorneth the scorners: but he giveth grace unto the lowly. *Proverbs 3:34*

By humility and the fear of the LORD are riches, and honour, and life. *Proverbs 22:4*

A man's pride shall bring him low: but honour shall uphold the humble in spirit.

Proverbs 29:23

For the LORD taketh pleasure in his people: he will beautify the meek with salvation.

Psalm 149:4

Sing praises to the LORD. . .

. . .he remembereth them: he forgetteth not the cry of the humble. *Psalm 9:11–12*

The fear of the LORD is the instruction of wis-dom; and before honour is humility.

Proverbs 15:33

Serving the Lord with all humility of mind. . .

Acts 20:19

JOY

No matter what frustrations and disappointments life brings us, still God has promised us a life full of joy.

These things have I spoken unto you, that my joy might remain in you, and that your joy might be full. *John 15:11*

Thou wilt shew me the path of life: in thy presence is fulness of joy; at thy right hand there are pleasures for evermore.
Psalm 16:11

Whom having not seen, ye love; in whom, though now ye see him not, yet believing, ye rejoice with joy unspeakable and full of glory. *1 Peter 1:8*

. . .Go your way, eat the fat, and drink the sweet, and send portions unto them for whom nothing is prepared: for this day is holy unto our Lord: neither be ye sorry; for the joy of the LORD is your strength.
Nehemiah 8:10

But let the righteous be glad; let them rejoice before God: yea, let them exceedingly rejoice. *Psalm 68:3*

Rejoice in the LORD alway: and again I say, Rejoice. *Philippians 4:4*

The righteous shall be glad in the LORD, and shall trust in him; and all the upright in heart shall glory.   *Psalm 64:10*

Yet I will rejoice in the LORD, I will joy in the God of my salvation.

The LORD God is my strength, and he will make my feet like hinds' feet, and he will make me to walk upon mine high places. . .
                                    Habakkuk 3:18–19

For ye shall go out with joy, and be led forth with peace: the mountains and the hills shall break forth before you into singing, and all the trees of the field shall clap their hands.
                                    Isaiah 55:12

I will greatly rejoice in the LORD, my soul shall be joyful in my God; for he hath clothed me with the garments of salvation, he hath covered me with the robe of righteousness, as a bridegroom decketh himself with ornaments, and as a bride adorneth herself with her jewels.   *Isaiah 61:10*

The voice of rejoicing and salvation is in the tabernacles of the righteous: the right hand of the LORD doeth valiantly.   *Psalm 118:15*

Thou hast put gladness in my heart, more than in the time that their corn and their wine increased.   *Psalm 4:7*

The light of the eyes rejoiceth the heart: and a good report maketh the bones fat.

Proverbs 15:30

. . .The Lord GOD will wipe away tears from off all faces. . .

And it shall be said in that day, Lo, this is our God; we have waited for him, and he will save us: this is the LORD; we have waited for him, we will be glad and rejoice in his salvation. *Isaiah 25:8–9*

Therefore the redeemed of the LORD shall return, and come with singing unto Zion; and everlasting joy shall be upon their head: they shall obtain gladness and joy; and sorrow and mourning shall flee away.

Isaiah 51:11

KINDNESS

In a cutthroat, get-ahead world, we are called to be kind to those around us, spreading Christ's love to the world.

Put on therefore, as the elect of God, holy and beloved, bowels of mercies, kindness, humbleness of mind, meekness, longsuffering;

Forbearing one another, and forgiving one another, if any man have a quarrel against any: even as Christ forgave you, so also do ye.   *Colossians 3:12–13*

But love ye your enemies, and do good, and lend, hoping for nothing again; and your reward shall be great, and ye shall be the children of the Highest: for he is kind unto the unthankful and to the evil. Be ye therefore merciful, as your Father also is merciful.
Luke 6:35

And beside this, giving all diligence, add to your faith virtue; and to virtue knowledge;

And to knowledge temperance; and to temperance patience; and to patience godliness;

And to godliness brotherly kindness; and to brotherly kindness charity.
2 Peter 1:5–7

Charity suffereth long, and is kind. . .
1 Corinthians 13:4

Who can find a virtuous woman? . . .

She openeth her mouth with wisdom; and in her tongue is the law of kindness.

Proverbs 31:10, 26

But in all thing approving ourselves as the ministers of God. . .

By pureness, by knowledge, by long-suffering, by kindness, by the Holy Ghost, by love unfeigned.   *2 Corinthians 6:4, 6*

Let love be without dissimulation. Abhor that which is evil; cleave to that which is good.

Be kindly affectioned one to another with brotherly love. . .   *Romans 12:9–10*

And be ye kind one to another, tender-hearted, forgiving one another, even as God for Christ's sake hath forgiven you.

Ephesians 4:32

KNOWLEDGE

The world puts a lot of emphasis on knowledge—but the Bible reminds us that worldly knowledge pales in comparison to the knowledge of God.

According as his divine power hath given unto us all things that pertain unto life and godliness, through the knowledge of him that hath called us to glory and virtue.

2 Peter 1:3

Hearken unto this, O Job: stand still, and consider the wondrous works of God. . . .

Dost thou know the balancings of the clouds, the wondrous works of him which is perfect in knowledge? *Job 37:14, 16*

My son, if thou wilt receive my words, and hide my commandments with thee. . .

Yea, if thou criest after knowledge, and liftest up thy voice for understanding; . . .

Then shalt thou understand the fear of the LORD, and find the knowledge of God.

Proverbs 2:1, 3, 5

But the manifestation of the Spirit is given to every man to profit withal.

For to one is given by the Spirit the word of wisdom; to another the word of knowledge by the same Spirit.

1 Corinthians 12:7–8

And though I have the gift of prophecy, and understand all mysteries, and all knowledge; and though I have all faith, so that I could remove mountains, and have not charity, I am nothing.   *1 Corinthians 13:2*

Now thanks be unto God, which always causeth us to triumph in Christ, and maketh manifest the savour of his knowledge by us in every place.   *2 Corinthians 2:14*

And thou, child, shalt be called the prophet of the Highest: for thou shalt go before the face of the Lord to prepare his ways;

To give knowledge of salvation unto his people by the remission of their sins.

Luke 1:76–77

All the words of my mouth are in righteousness; there is nothing froward or perverse in them.

They are all plain to him that understandeth, and right to them that find knowledge.

Proverbs 8:8–9

And I gave my heart to know wisdom, and to know madness and folly: I perceived that this also is vexation of spirit.

For in much wisdom is much grief: and he that increaseth knowledge increaseth sorrow.   *Ecclesiastes 1:17–18*

For God giveth to a man that is good in his sight wisdom, and knowledge, and joy: but to the sinner he giveth travail, to gather and to heap up, that he may give to him that is good before God. This also is vanity and vexation of spirit.

Ecclesiastes 2:26

. . .If ye continue in my word, then are ye my disciples indeed;

And ye shall know the truth, and the truth shall make you free.

John 8:31–32

But continue thou in the things which thou hast learned and hast been assured of, knowing of whom thou hast learned them;

And that from a child thou hast known the holy scriptures, which are able to make thee wise unto salvation through faith which is in Christ Jesus.   *2 Timothy 3:14–15*

Ye therefore, beloved, seeing ye know these things. . .

. . .grow in grace, and in the knowledge of our Lord and Saviour Jesus Christ.

2 Peter 3:17–18

O the depth of the riches both of the wisdom and knowledge of God! how unsearchable are his judgments, and his ways past finding out!   *Romans 11:33*

Be still, and know that I am God. . .

Psalm 46:10

For this cause we also, since the day we heard it, do not cease to pray for you, and to desire that ye might be filled with the knowledge of his will in all wisdom and spiritual understanding;

That ye might walk worthy of the Lord unto all pleasing, being fruitful in every good work, and increasing in the knowledge of God. *Colossians 1:9–10*

. . .I am not ashamed: for I know whom I have believed. . . *2 Timothy 1:12*

And if any man think that he knoweth any thing, he knoweth nothing yet as he ought to know.

But if any man love God, the same is known of him. *1 Corinthians 8:2–3*

LONELINESS

Being single can be a blessing, but it can also be lonely. No matter where we go, though, we can rest in the knowledge that God goes with us. He is our companion on life's journey.

For in him [Christ] dwelleth all the fulness of the Godhead bodily.

And ye are complete in him. . .
Colossians 2:9–10

I will not leave you comfortless: I will come to you.

Yet a little while, and the world seeth me no more; but ye see me: because I live, ye shall live also.   *John 14:18–19*

Hide not thy face far from me; put not thy servant away in anger: thou hast been my help; leave me not, neither forsake me, O God of my salvation.

When my father and my mother forsake me, then the LORD will take me up.
Psalm 27:9–10

. . .Fear not: for I have redeemed thee, I have called thee by thy name; thou art mine.

When thou passest through the waters, I will be with thee. . .

Fear not: for I am with thee.
Isaiah 43:1–2, 5

And, behold, I am with thee, and will keep thee in all places whither thou goest. . .

Genesis 28:15

. . .As I was with Moses, so I will be with thee: I will not fail thee nor forsake thee.

Joshua 1:5

Therefore is my spirit overwhelmed within me; my heart within me is desolate. . . .

Hear me speedily, O LORD: my spirit faileth: hide not thy face from me. . .

Cause me to hear thy lovingkindness in the morning; for in thee do I trust. . .

Psalm 143:4, 7–8

The LORD also will be a refuge for the oppressed, a refuge in times of trouble.

And they that know thy name will put their trust in thee: for thou, LORD, hast not forsaken them that seek thee.

Psalm 9:9–10

Can a woman forget her sucking child, that she should not have compassion on the son of her womb? yea, they may forget, yet will I not forget thee.

Behold, I have graven thee upon the palms of my hands; thy walls are continually before me. *Isaiah 49:15–16*

For I am with thee, saith the LORD, to save thee. . . *Jeremiah 30:11*

Fear thou not; for I am with thee: be not dismayed; for I am thy God: I will strengthen thee; yea, I will help thee; yea, I will uphold thee with the right hand of my righteousness.

Isaiah 41:10

. . .Thou art with me. . .   *Psalm 23:4*

Then shalt thou call, and the LORD shall answer; thou shalt cry, and he shall say, Here I am. . .   *Isaiah 58:9*

. . .Be content with such things as ye have: for he hath said, I will never leave thee, nor forsake thee.

So that we may boldly say, The LORD is my helper. . .   *Hebrews 13:5–6*

Be strong and of a good courage, fear not, nor be afraid of them: for the LORD thy God, he it is that doth go with thee; he will not fail thee, nor forsake thee.

Deuteronomy 31:6

LONGING

As single people, sometimes our hearts are full of longing. God understands our hearts, though, and this too we can give to Him.

Delight thyself also in the LORD; and he shall give thee the desires of thine heart.

Psalm 37:4

For he satisfieth the longing soul, and filleth the hungry soul with goodness.

Psalm 107:9

Thou openest thine hand, and saitsifiest the desire of every living thing. *Psalm 145:16*

What man is there of you whom, if his son ask bread, will he give him a stone? . . .

If ye then, being evil, know how to give good gifts unto your children, how much more shall your Father, who is in heaven, give good things to them that ask him?

Matthew 7:9, 11

. . .They who seek the LORD shall not lack any good thing. *Psalm 34:10*

They shall not hunger nor thirst; neither shall the heat nor sun smite them: for he that hath mercy on them shall lead them, even by the springs of water shall he guide them.

Isaiah 49:10

And I will set up shepherds over them which shall feed them: and they shall fear no more, nor be dismayed, neither shall they be lacking, saith the LORD.   *Jeremiah 23:4*

His mercy is on them.. . .
　　He hath filled the hungry with good things. . .   *Luke 1:50, 53*

Oh that I might have my request; and that God would grant me the thing that I long for!   *Job 6:8*

He turneth the wilderness into a standing water, and dry ground into watersprings.
　　And there he maketh the hungry to dwell. . .   *Psalm 107:35–36*

Ho, every one that thirsteth, come ye to the waters, and he that hath no money; come ye, buy, and eat; yea, come, buy wine and milk without money and without price.
　　Wherefore do ye spend money for that which is not bread? and your labour for that which satisfieth not? hearken diligently unto me, and eat ye that which is good, and let your soul delight itself in fatness.
　　　　　　　　　　Isaiah 55:1–2

Blessed are they which do hunger and thirst after righteousness: for they shall be filled.
　　　　　　　　　　Matthew 5:6

MARRIAGE

No doubt about it, marriage is a blessing from God. Being single can also be a blessing too, however, and we need to trust God to lead us by whatever path is truly best for us and for God's kingdom.

But I would have you without carefulness. He that is unmarried careth for the things that belong to the Lord, how he may please the Lord:

But he that is married careth for the things that are of the world, how he may please his wife. . . .

The unmarried woman careth for the things of the Lord, that she may be holy both in body and in spirit: but she that is married careth for the things of the world, how she may please her husband.

And this I speak for your own profit. . . that ye may attend upon the Lord without distraction. *1 Corinthians 7:32–35*

Sing, O barren, thou that didst not bear; break forth into singing, and cry aloud, thou that didst not travail with child: for more are the children of the desolate than the children of the married wife, saith the LORD.

Isaiah 54:1

And the LORD God said, "It is not good that the man should be alone; I will make him an help meet for him." *Genesis 2:18*

House and riches are the inheritance of fathers: and a prudent wife is from the LORD.
Proverbs 19:14

Two are better than one; because they have a good reward for their labour.

For if they fall, the one will lift up his fellow: but woe to him that is alone when he falleth; for he hath not another to help him up.

Again, if two lie together, then they have heat: but how can one be warm alone?

And if one prevail against him, two shall withstand him; and a threefold cord is not quickly broken. *Ecclesiastes 4:9–12*

PEACE

Our lives are so full of responsibilities and relationships and activities, that sometimes we don't have much peace. When we rely on God to direct each aspect of our life, though, then even when we are in the midst of turmoil, He gives us His peace.

Mark the perfect man, and behold the upright: for the end of that man is peace.

Psalm 37:37

Those things, which ye have both learned, and received, and heard, and seen in me, do: and the God of peace shall be with you.

Philippians 4:9

And the very God of peace sanctify you wholly; and I pray God your whole spirit and soul and body be preserved blameless unto the coming of our Lord Jesus Christ.

Faithful is he that calleth you, who also will do it.   *1 Thessalonians 5:23–24*

For the mountains shall depart, and the hills be removed; but my kindness shall not depart from thee, neither shall the covenant of my peace be removed, saith the LORD that hath mercy on thee.   *Isaiah 54:10*

For ye shall go out with joy, and be led forth with peace. . .   *Isaiah 55:12*

But the meek shall inherit the earth; and shall delight themselves in the abundance of peace. *Psalm 37:11*

When a man's ways please the LORD, he maketh even his enemies to be at peace with him. *Proverbs 16:7*

Peace I leave with you, my peace I give unto you: not as the world giveth, give I unto you. Let not your heart be troubled, neither let it be afraid. *John 14:27*

Thou wilt keep him in perfect peace, whose mind is stayed on thee: because he trusteth in thee. *Isaiah 26:3*

Therefore being justified by faith, we have peace with God through our Lord Jesus Christ. *Romans 5:1*

For to be carnally minded is death; but to be spiritually minded is life and peace.
Romans 8:6

Great peace have they which love thy law: and nothing shall offend them.
Psalm 119:165

For the kingdom of God is not meat and drink; but righteousness, and peace, and joy in the Holy Ghost. *Romans 14:17*

These things have I spoken unto you, that in me ye might have peace. In the world ye shall have tribulation: but be of good cheer; I have overcome the world. *John 16:33*

. . .Be of one mind, live in peace; and the God of love and peace shall be with you.
2 Corinthians 13:11

. . .Peace, peace be unto thee, and peace be to thine helpers; for thy God helpeth thee. . . .
1 Chronicles 12:18

. . .The God of peace shall be with you.
Philippians 4:9

PERSEVERING

It's hard to stick to something that's not easy. Too often we run from thing to thing, never really committing ourselves, giving up whenever things seem too hard. God calls us to persevere in our walk with Him, though, to keep on trying, no matter how hard things may be. And when we do, He richly blesses us.

Better is the end of a thing than the beginning thereof: and the patient in spirit is better than the proud in spirit.   *Ecclesiastes 7:8*

Rest in the LORD, and wait patiently for him: fret not thyself because of him who prospereth in his way, because of the man who bringeth wicked devices to pass.
Psalm 37:7

Because thou hast kept the word of my patience, I also will keep thee from the hour of temptation, which shall come upon all the world, to try them that dwell upon the earth.
Revelation 3:10

And we desire that every one of you do shew the same diligence to the full assurance of hope unto the end:

That ye be not slothful, but followers of them who through faith and patience inherit the promises.   *Hebrews 6:11–12*

I waited patiently for the LORD; and he inclined unto me, and heard my cry.

Psalm 40:1

Be patient therefore, brethren, unto the coming of the Lord. Behold, the husbandman waiteth for the precious fruit of the earth, and hath long patience for it, until he receive the early and latter rain.

Be ye also patient; stablish your hearts: for the coming of the Lord draweth nigh.

James 5:7–8

Cast not away therefore your confidence, which hath great recompence of reward.

For ye have need of patience, that, after ye have done the will of God, ye might receive the promise.

For yet a little while, and he that shall come will come, and will not tarry.

Hebrews 10:35–37

Wherefore seeing we also are compassed about with so great a cloud of witnesses, let us lay aside every weight, and the sin which doth so easily beset us, and let us run with patience the race that is set before us,

Looking unto Jesus the author and finisher of our faith; who for the joy that was set before him endured the cross, despising the shame, and is set down at the right hand of the throne of God. *Hebrews 12:1–2*

My brethren, count it all joy when ye fall into divers temptations;

Knowing this, that the trying of your faith worketh patience.

But let patience have her perfect work, that ye may be perfect and entire, wanting nothing.   *James 1:2–4*

And not only so, but we glory in tribulations also: knowing that tribulation worketh patience;

And patience, experience; and experience, hope.   *Romans 5:3–4*

And take the helmet of salvation, and the sword of the Spirit, which is the word of God:

Praying always with all prayer and supplication in the Spirit, and watching thereunto with all perseverance and supplication for all saints.   *Ephesians 6:17–18*

PRAYER

God speaks to us through His Word. Prayer is the way that we communicate back. If we are to have a true relationship with God, we need to spend time in both sides of this heavenly conversation.

Hear my prayer, O LORD, and let my cry come unto thee. *Psalm 102:1*

Continue in prayer, and watch in the same with thanksgiving. *Colossians 4:2*

For the eyes of the Lord are over the righteous, and his ears are open unto their prayers. . .
1 Peter 3:12

And the prayer of faith shall save the sick. . .
James 5:15

. . .I will pray with the spirit, and I will pray with the understanding also. . .
1 Corinthians 14:15

Is any among you afflicted? let him pray. . . .
. . .pray one for another, that ye may be healed. The effectual fervent prayer of a righteous man availeth much.
James 5:13, 16

Pray without ceasing.
1 Thessalonians 5:17

He will regard the prayer of the destitute, and not despise their prayer.

Psalm 102:17

. . .I give myself unto prayer. *Psalm 109:4*

I will therefore that men pray every where, lifting up holy hands, without wrath and doubting. *1 Timothy 2:8*

If my people, which are called by my name, shall humble themselves, and pray, and seek my face, and turn from their wicked ways; then will I hear from heaven, and will forgive their sin, and will heal their land.

2 Chronicles 7:14

Hearken unto the voice of my cry, my King, and my God: for unto thee will I pray.

My voice shalt thou hear in the morning, O LORD; in the morning will I direct my prayer unto thee, and will look up.

Psalm 5:2–3

. . .Pray unto the LORD for it: for in the peace thereof shall ye have peace. . . .

Then shall ye call upon me, and ye shall go and pray unto me, and I will hearken unto you.

And ye shall seek me, and find me, when ye shall search for me with all your heart.

Jeremiah 29:7, 12–13

. . .Pray for them which despitefully use you, and persecute you.   *Matthew 5:44*

But thou, when thou prayest, enter into thy closet, and when thou hast shut thy door, pray to thy Father which is in secret; and thy Father which seeth in secret shall reward thee openly.   *Matthew 6:6*

Be careful for nothing; but in every thing by prayer and supplication with thanksgiving let your requests be made known unto God.
Philippians 4:6

After this manner therefore pray ye: Our Father which art in heaven, Hallowed be thy name.

Thy kingdom come. Thy will be done in earth, as it is in heaven.

Give us this day our daily bread.

And forgive us our debts, as we forgive our debtors.

And lead us not into temptation, but deliver us from evil: For thine is the kingdom, and the power, and the glory, for ever. Amen.
Matthew 6:9–13

PRUDENCE

The Bible calls us to live our lives prudently, with care and wisdom, rather than carelessly, doing whatever comes easiest. Remember, when the world looks at us, they should see Christ.

A prudent man concealeth knowledge; but the heart of fools proclaimeth foolishness.

Proverbs 12:23

For wisdom is better than rubies; and all the things that may be desired are not to be compared to it.

I wisdom dwell with prudence. . . .

Proverbs 8:11–12

The wisdom of the prudent is to understand his way: but the folly of fools is deceit.

Proverbs 14:8

The wise in heart shall be called prudent: and the sweetness of the lips increaseth learning.

Proverbs 16:21

A fool despiseth his father's instruction: but he that regardeth reproof is prudent.

Proverbs 15:5

The simple believeth every word: but the prudent man looketh well to his going.

Proverbs 14:15

The simple inherit folly: but the prudent are crowned with knowledge.

Proverbs 14:18

The way of a fool is right in his own eyes: but he that hearkeneth unto counsel is wise.

A fool's wrath is presently known: but a prudent man covereth shame.

Proverbs 12:15–16

Every prudent man dealeth with knowledge: but a fool layeth open his folly.

Proverbs 13:16

The heart of the prudent getteth knowledge; and the ear of the wise seeketh knowledge.

Proverbs 18:15

PURITY

Sometimes the word pure almost seems like a negative concept, as though it contains a long list of can'ts and don'ts. In reality, though, if we are pure, then we are not weakened by anything, not mixed up with something that's not real. Just as pure gold is gold that is undiluted by any less precious substance, we are called to be pure Christians. The world holds many temptations—but we do not want to dilute or weaken Christ's indwelling Spirit.

Finally brethren, whatsoever things are true, whatsoever things are honest, whatsoever things are just, whatsoever things are pure, whatsoever things are lovely, whatsoever things are of good report; if there be any virtue, and if there be any praise, think on these things. *Philippians 4:8*

Blessed are the pure in heart: for they shall see God. *Matthew 5:8*

. . .All things indeed are pure; but it is evil for that man who eateth with offence.

It is good neither to eat flesh, nor to drink wine, nor any thing whereby they brother stumbleth, or is offended, or is made weak. *Romans 14:20–21*

Thy word is very pure: therefore thy servant loveth it. *Psalm 119:140*

The thoughts of the wicked are an abomination to the LORD: but the words of the pure are pleasant words.

Proverbs 15:26

Unto the pure all things are pure: but unto them that are defiled and unbelieving is nothing pure; but even their mind and conscience is defiled.

Titus 1:15

Let us draw near with a true heart in full assurance of faith, having our hearts sprinkled from an evil conscience, and our bodies washed with pure water.

Hebrews 10:22

The words of the LORD are pure words: as silver tried in a furnace of earth, purified seven times.

Psalm 12:6

REPENTANCE

We all make mistakes; sooner or later, all of us fall into sin, and then we need to repent. True repentance means we will examine our lives, feel sorry for our mistakes—and then with God's help we will change.

The Lord is not slack concerning his promise, as some men count slackness; but is longsuffering to us–ward, not willing that any should perish, but that all should come to repentance.   *2 Peter 3:9*

Now I rejoice, not that ye were made sorry, but that ye sorrowed to repentance: for ye were made sorry after a godly manner. . .

For godly sorrow worketh repentance to salvation not to be repented of: but the sorrow of the world worketh death.
                                    2 Corinthians 7:9–10

Have mercy upon me, O God, according to they lovingkindness: according unto the multitude of thy tender mercies blot out my transgressions.

Wash me thoroughly from mine iniquity, and cleanse me from my sin.

For I acknowledge my transgressions: and my sin is ever before me.

Against thee, thee only, have I sinned. . .

Purge me with hyssop, and I shall be clean: wash me, and I shall be whiter than snow.   *Psalm 51:1–4, 7*

. . .Thus it behoved Christ to suffer. . .

That repentance and remission of sins should be preached in his name among all nations. . .   *Luke 24:46–47*

The LORD is nigh unto them that are of a broken heart; and saveth such as be of a contrite spirit.   *Psalm 34:18*

If iniquity be in thine hand, put it far away, and let not wickedness dwell in thy tabernacles.

For then shalt thou lift up thy face without spot; yea, thou shalt be stedfast, and shalt not fear.   *Job 11:14–15*

SELF-CONCEPT

Sometimes it's hard to feel good about ourselves. We try so hard to measure up to the world's standards of what we should look like, how we should dress, how much money we should make, how much education we should have—and the list goes on. We need to remember that we don't have to work to make ourselves attractive in God's eyes. Our self-concepts should be firmly based in Christ's redeeming love: He delights in us just as we are.

Thou shalt no more be termed Forsaken; neither shall thy land any more be termed Desolate: but thou shalt be called Hephzibah, and thy land Beulah: for the LORD delighteth in thee. . .   *Isaiah 62:4*

Thou art beautiful, O my love, as Tirzah, comely as Jerusalem, terrible as an army with banners.   *Song of Solomon 6:4*

O thou afflicted, tossed with tempest, and not comforted, behold, I will lay thy stones with fair colours, and lay thy foundations with sapphires.   *Isaiah 54:11*

I will praise thee; for I am fearfully and wonderfully made: marvellous are thy works; and that my soul knoweth right well.
Psalm 139:14

Thou art fairer than the children of men: grace is poured into thy lips: therefore God hath blessed thee for ever. *Psalm 45:2*

Behold, thou art fair, my love; behold, thou art fair. . . *Song of Solomon 1:15*

My beloved spake, and said unto me, Rise up, my love, my fair one, and come away.

For, lo, the winter is past, the rain is over and gone;

The flowers appear on the earth; the time of the singing of birds is come, and the voice of the turtle is heard in our land;

The fig tree putteth forth her green figs, and the vines with the tender grape give a good smell. Arise, my love, my fair one, and come away. *Song of Solomon 2:10–13*

SELF-CONTROL

The philosophy of the world tells us to do whatever feels good, whatever comes easiest—but the Bible calls us to a life of self-control.

Ye have heard that it hath been said, An eye for an eye, and a tooth for a tooth:

But I say unto you, That ye resist not evil: but whosoever shall smite thee on thy right cheek, turn to him the other also.

Matthew 5:38–39

And they that are Christ's have crucified the flesh with the affections and lusts.

If we live in the Spirit, let us also walk in the Spirit. *Galatians 5:24–25*

For the grace of God that bringeth salvation hath appeared to all men,

Teaching us that, denying ungodliness and worldly lusts, we should live soberly, righteously, and godly, in this present world.

Titus 2:11–12

And when the tempter came to him. . .

He answered and said, "It is written, Man shall not live by bread alone, but by every word that proceedeth out of the mouth of God." *Matthew 4:3–4*

In your patience possess ye your souls.

Luke 21:19

But be ye doers of the word, and not hearers only, deceiving your own selves.

James 1:22

Therefore, brethren, we are debtors, not to the flesh, to live after the flesh.

For if ye live after the flesh, ye shall die: but if ye through the Spirit do mortify the deeds of the body, ye shall live.

Romans 8:12–13

Then said Jesus unto his disciples, "If any man will come after me, let him deny himself, and take up his cross, and follow me.

For whosoever will save his life shall lose it: and whosoever will lose his life for my sake shall find it." *Matthew 16:24–25*

Now we exhort you, brethren, warn them that are unruly, comfort the feebleminded, support the weak, be patient toward all men.

See that none render evil for evil unto any man; but ever follow that which is good, both among yourselves, and to all men.

1 Thessalonians 5:14–15

There hath no temptation taken you but such as is common to man: but God is faithful, who will not suffer you to be tempted above that ye are able; but will with the temptation also make a way to escape, that ye may be able to bear it. *1 Corinthians 10:13*

For even hereunto were ye called: because Christ also suffered for us, leaving us an example, that ye should follow his steps:

Who did no sin, neither was guile found in his mouth:

Who, when he was reviled, reviled not again; when he suffered, he threatened not; but committed himself to him that judgeth righteously.   *1 Peter 2:21–23*

And that ye study to be quiet, and to do your own business, and to work with your own hands, as we commanded you;

That ye may walk honestly. . .
                    1 Thessalonians 4:11–12

But let us, who are of the day, be sober, putting on the breastplate of faith and love. . .
                    1 Thessalonians 5:8

SERENITY

No matter what tensions our life holds, God's Spirit gives us an indestructable serenity.

There remaineth therefore a rest to the people of God.

For he that is entered into his rest, he also hath ceased from his own works, as God did from his. *Hebrews 4:9–10*

Return unto thy rest, O my soul; for the LORD hath dealt bountifully with thee.

For thou hast delivered my soul from death, mine eyes from tears, and my feet from falling. *Psalm 116:7–8*

For thus saith the Lord GOD, the Holy One of Israel; In returning and rest shall ye be saved; in quietness and in confidence shall be your strength. . . *Isaiah 30:15*

He maketh the storm a calm, so that the waves thereof are still.

Then are they glad because they be quiet; so he bringeth them unto their desired haven. *Psalm 107:29–30*

But they that wait upon the LORD shall renew their strength; they shall mount up with wings as eagles; they shall run, and not be weary; and they shall walk, and not faint.

Isaiah 40:31

He that dwelleth in the secret place of the most High shall abide under the shadow of the Almighty. . . .

Because thou hast made the LORD, which is my refuge, even the most High, thy habitation;

There shall no evil befall thee, neither shall any plague come nigh thy dwelling.

Psalm 91:1, 9–10

But whoso hearkeneth unto me shall dwell safely, and shall be quiet from fear of evil.

Proverbs 1:33

Rest in the LORD, and wait patiently for him: fret not thyself because of him who prospereth in his way, because of the man who bringeth wicked devices to pass.

Psalm 37:7

SINCERITY

A person who is sincere is genuine and wholehearted, not two-faced or hypocritical. The people we talk with should be able to see in our sincerity that Christ lives in us, making us different from those around us.

Wherefore laying aside all malice, and all guile, and hypocrisies, and envies, and all evil speakings,

As newborn babes, desire the sincere milk of the word, that ye may grow thereby:

If so be ye have tasted that the Lord is gracious. *1 Peter 2:1–3*

For even Christ our passover is sacrificed for us:

Therefore let us keep the feast, not with old leaven, neither with the leaven of malice and wickedness; but with the unleavened bread of sincerity and truth.

1 Corinthians 5:7–8

Now therefore fear the LORD, and serve him in sincerity and in truth: and put away the gods which your fathers served on the other side of the flood, and in Egypt; and serve ye the LORD. *Joshua 24:14*

In all things shewing thyself a pattern of good works: in doctrine shewing uncorruptness, gravity, sincerity. *Titus 2:7*

For our rejoicing is this, the testimony of our conscience, that in simplicity and godly sincerity, not with fleshly wisdom, but by the grace of God, we have had our conversation in the world, and more abundantly to you-ward.   *2 Corinthians 1:12*

That ye may approve things that are excellent; that ye may be sincere and without offence till the day of Christ;

Being filled with the fruits of righteousness, which are by Jesus Christ, unto the glory and praise of God.   *Philippians 1:10–11*

Grace be with all them that love our Lord Jesus Christ in sincerity. Amen.

Ephesians 6:24

SINGLEMINDEDNESS

So many things in life try to get our attention, distracting us from Christ. The Bible reminds us, though, that we are to keep our eyes fixed on Jesus, "the author and finisher of our faith" (Hebrews 12:2).

The light of the body is the eye: if therefore thine eye be single, thy whole body shall be full of light.

But if thine eye be evil, thy whole body shall be full of darkness. If therefore the light that is in thee be darkness, how great is that darkness!

Matthew 6:22–23

And all that believed were together, and had all things common;

. . .continuing daily with one accord in the temple. . .did eat their meat with gladness and singleness of heart,

Praising God, and having favour with all the people. . . *Acts 2:44, 46–47*

What? Know ye not that your body is the temple of the Holy Ghost which is in you, which ye have of God, and ye are not your own?

For ye are bought with a price: therefore glorify God in your body, and in your spirit, which are God's.

1 Corinthians 6:19–20

For the eyes of the LORD run to and fro throughout the whole earth, to shew himself strong in the behalf of them whose heart is perfect toward him. . .   *2 Chronicles 16:9*

For where your treasure is, there will your heart be also.

The light of the body is the eye: if therefore thine eye be single, thy whole body shall be full of light.   *Matthew 6:21–22*

. . .Be obedient to them that are your masters according to the flesh, with fear and trembling, in singleness of your heart, as unto Christ;

Not with eyeservice, as menpleasers; but as the servants of Christ, doing the will of God from the heart.   *Ephesians 6:5–6*

SUCCESS

Our culture values success when it comes to financial gain and professional advancement. We need to keep in mind, though, that true success comes only from God.

This book of the law shall not depart out of thy mouth; but thou shalt meditate therein day and night, that thou mayest observe to do according to all that is written therein: for then thou shalt make thy way prosperous, and then thou shalt have good success.
Joshua 1:8

Unto thee, O LORD, do I lift up my soul.

O my God, I trust in thee: let me not be ashamed, let not mine enemies triumph over me.   *Psalm 25:1–2*

. . .They shall prosper that love thee.

Peace be within thy walls, and prosperity within thy palaces.   *Psalm 122:6–7*

Beloved, I wish above all things that thou mayest prosper and be in health, even as thy soul prospereth.   *3 John 2*

Therefore, my beloved brethren, be ye stedfast, unmoveable, always abounding in the work of the Lord, forasmuch as ye know that your labour is not in vain in the Lord.
1 Corinthians 15:58

. . .Blessed is the man that feareth the LORD, that delighteth greatly in his commandments. . . .

Wealth and riches shall be in his house: and his righteousness endureth for ever.

Psalm 112:1, 3

Only be thou strong and very courageous, that thou mayest observe to do according to all the law, which Moses my servant commanded thee: turn not from it to the right hand or to the left, that thou mayest prosper whithersoever thou goest.

Joshua 1:7

. . .The God of heaven, he will prosper us; therefore we his servants will arise and build. . .   *Nehemiah 2:20*

TEACHABLE

Most of us have worked hard to get where we are today. In the process, we have learned a great deal—but the Bible reminds us that we will always have more to learn. We should not be "know-it-alls" but instead be receptive to what God wants to teach us.

And thou shalt speak unto him, and put words in his mouth; and I will be with thy mouth, and with his mouth, and will teach you what ye shall do.   *Exodus 4:15*

Good and upright is the LORD: therefore will he teach sinners in the way.

The meek will he guide in judgment: and the meek will he teach his way.
Psalm 25:8–9

Come, ye children, hearken unto me: I will teach you the fear of the LORD.

What man is he that desireth life, and loveth many days, that he may see good?

Keep thy tongue from evil, and thy lips from speaking guile.

Depart from evil, and do good; seek peace, and pursue it.   *Psalm 34:11–14*

And Jesus, when he came out, saw much people, and was moved with compassion toward them, because they were as sheep not having a shepherd: and he began to teach them many things.   *Mark 6:34*

Teach me, and I will hold my tongue: and cause me to understand wherein I have erred.

Job 6:24

I will instruct thee and teach thee in the way which thou shalt go: I will guide thee with mine eye.

Be ye not as the horse, or as the mule, which have no understanding: whose mouth must be held in with bit and bridle, lest they come near unto thee.

Psalm 32:8–9

Teach me to do thy will; for thou art my God: thy spirit is good; lead me into the land of uprightness.

Psalm 143:10

And when they bring you unto the synagogues, and unto magistrates, and powers, take ye no thought how or what thing ye shall answer, or what ye shall say:

For the Holy Ghost shall teach you in the same hour what ye ought to say.

Luke 12:11–12

And though the Lord give you the bread of adversity, and the water of affliction, yet shall not thy teachers be removed into a corner any more, but thine eyes shall see thy teachers:

And thine ears shall hear a word behind thee, saying, This is the way, walk ye in it, when ye turn to the right hand, and when ye turn to the left.

Isaiah 30:20–21

Blessed art thou, O LORD: teach me thy statutes. . .

I have declared my ways, and thou heardest me: teach me thy statutes. . . .

Teach me good judgment and knowledge: for I have believed thy commandments.   *Psalm 119:12, 26, 66*

Now we have received, not the spirit of the world, but the spirit which is of God; that we might know the things that are freely given to us of God.

Which things also we speak, not in the words which man's wisdom teacheth, but which the Holy Ghost teacheth; comparing spiritual things with spiritual.

1 Corinthians 2:12–13

The heart of the wise teacheth his mouth, and addeth learning to his lips.

Proverbs 16:23

TEMPERANCE

If we are temperate, then we restrain ourselves from going to extremes. We stick to the middle of the road, controlling our tempers, staying calm, and pressing on to our goal: Christ Jesus.

And they that are Christ's have crucified the flesh with the affections and lusts.

If we live in the Spirit, let us also walk in the Spirit.   *Galatians 5:24–25*

. . .Giving all diligence, add to your faith virtue; and to virtue knowledge;

And to knowledge temperance; and to temperance patience. . .   *2 Peter 1:5–6*

And every man that striveth for the mastery is temperate in all things. . . . .

I therefore so run, not as uncertainly; so fight I, not as one that beateth the air:

But I keep under my body, and bring it into subjection: lest that by any means, when I have preached to others, I myself should be a castaway.   *1 Corinthians 9:25–27*

For the grace of God that bringeth salvation hath appeared to all men,

Teaching us that, denying ungodliness and worldly lusts, we should live soberly, righteously, and godly, in this present world.
     Titus 2:11–12

Let your moderation be known unto all men. . . .   *Philippians 4:5*

Thou therefore endure hardness, as a good soldier of Jesus Christ.

No man that warreth entangleth himself with the affairs of this life; that he may please him who hath chosen him to be a soldier.

2 Timothy 2:3–4

TRUST

Trust in God is the way we reach out and take the good things He offers. Trust enables us to walk in hope, knowing that God will keep His promises.

Thou wilt keep him in perfect peace, whose mind is stayed on thee: because he trusteth in thee.

Trust ye in the Lord for ever: for in the Lord Je-ho-vah is everlasting strength.

Isaiah 26:3–4

Be merciful unto me, O God, be merciful unto me: for my soul trusteth in thee: yea, in the shadow of thy wings will I make my refuge, until these calamities be overpast.

Psalm 57:1

It is better to trust in the Lord than to put confidence in man.

It is better to trust in the Lord than to put confidence in princes. *Psalm 118:8–9*

They that trust in the Lord shall be as mount Zion, which cannot be removed, but abideth for ever. *Psalm 125:1*

The God of my rock; in him will I trust: he is my shield, and the horn of my salvation, my high tower, and my refuge, my saviour; thou savest me from violence.

2 Samuel 22:3

For after this manner in the old time the holy women also. . .trusted in God.   *1 Peter 3:5*

Many sorrows shall be to the wicked: but he that trusteth in the LORD, mercy shall compass him about.   *Psalm 32:10*

The eternal God is thy refuge, and underneath are the everlasting arms: and he shall thrust out the enemy from before thee. . .
   Deuteronomy 33:27

As for God, his way is perfect; the word of the LORD is tried: he is a buckler to all them that trust in him.   *2 Samuel 22:31*

But I am like a green olive tree in the house of God: I trust in the mercy of God for ever and ever.   *Psalm 52:8*

Some trust in chariots, and some in horses: but we will remember the name of the LORD our God.   *Psalm 20:7*

He shall cover thee with his feathers, and under his wings shalt thou trust: his truth shall be thy shield and buckler.
   Psalm 91:4

He shall not be afraid of evil tidings: his heart is fixed, trusting in the LORD.
His heart is established, he shall not be afraid. . .   *Psalm 112:7–8*

But I trusted in thee, O LORD: I said, Thou art my God.

My times are in thy hand: deliver me from the hand of mine enemies, and from them that persecute me.

Make thy face to shine upon thy servant: save me for thy mercies' sake. . . .

Oh how great is thy goodness, which thou hast laid up for them that fear thee; which thou hast wrought for them that trust in thee before the sons of men!

Psalm 31:14–16, 19

O taste and see that the LORD is good: blessed is the man that trusteth in him. . . .

The Lord redeemeth the soul of his servants: and none of them that trust in him shall be desolate. *Psalm 34:8, 22*

Behold, God is my salvation; I will trust, and not be afraid: for the LORD JEHOVAH is my strength and my song; he also is become my salvation. *Isaiah 12:2*

But we had the sentence of death in ourselves, that we should not trust in ourselves, but in God which raiseth the dead:

Who delivered us from so great a death, and doth deliver: in whom we trust that he will yet deliver us. *2 Corinthians 1:9–10*

Though he slay me, yet will I trust in him. . . *Job 13:15*

The righteous shall be glad in the LORD, and shall trust in him; and all the upright in heart shall glory. *Psalm 64:10*

Trust in the LORD, and do good; so shalt thou dwell in the land, and verily thou shalt be fed. *Psalm 37:3*

UPRIGHTNESS

Our world takes dishonesty lightly, and even "good" people lie. How easily we are influenced by this outlook—but the Bible calls us to walk uprightly and with integrity.

Unto the upright there ariseth light in the darkness: he is gracious, and full of compassion, and righteous. *Psalm 112:4*

I was also upright before him, and have kept myself from mine iniquity. . . .

With the merciful thou wilt shew thyself merciful, and with the upright man thou wilt shew thyself upright.

2 Samuel 22:24, 26

For the upright shall dwell in the land, and the perfect shall remain in it.

Proverbs 2:21

Keep back thy servant also from presumptuous sins; let them not have dominion over me: then shall I be upright, and I shall be innocent from the great transgression.

Psalm 19:13

The LORD knoweth the days of the upright: and their inheritance shall be for ever. . . .

Mark the perfect man, and behold the upright: for the end of that man is peace.

Psalm 37:18, 37

VANITY

The things of the world that are vain are those things that are empty and useless. When we put too much importance on the world thinks highly of us, that is one form of vanity. Another is if we think too highly of ourselves. Remember, we are to have the mind of Christ, valuing the things that truly matter.

Favour is deceitful, and beauty is vain. . .
Proverbs 31:30

Two things have I required of thee; deny me them not before I die:

Remove far from me vanity and lies: give me neither poverty nor riches; feed me with food convenient for me:

Lest I be full, and deny thee, and say, Who is the LORD: or lest I be poor, and steal, and take the name of my God in vain.
Proverbs 30:7–9

. . .We also are men of like passions with you, and preach unto you that ye should turn from these vanities unto the living God, which made heaven, and earth, and the sea, and all things that are therein.   *Acts 14:15*

Then I looked on all the works that my hands had wrought, and on the labour that I had laboured to do: and, behold, all was vanity and vexation of spirit, and there was no profit under the sun.   *Ecclesiastes 2:11*

The way of the LORD is strength to the upright: but destruction shall be to the workers of iniquity. *Proverbs 10:29*

He that walketh righteously, and speaketh uprightly; he that despiseth the gain of oppressions. . .and shutteth his eyes from seeing evil;

He shall dwell on high: his place of defence shall be the munitions of rocks: bread shall be given him; his waters shall be sure. *Isaiah 33:15–16*

The house of the wicked shall be overthrown: but the tabernacle of the upright shall flourish. *Proverbs 14:11*

Do good, O LORD, unto those that be good, and to them that are upright in their hearts. *Psalm 125:4*

The integrity of the upright shall guide them: but the perverseness of transgressors shall destroy them. . . .

The righteousness of the upright shall deliver them: but transgressors shall be taken in their own naughtiness. *Proverbs 11:3, 6*

The words of the wicked are to lie in wait for blood: but the mouth of the upright shall deliver them. *Proverbs 12:6*

. . .Knowledge puffeth up, but charity edifieth.

And if any man think that he knoweth any thing, he knoweth nothing yet as he ought to know.   *1 Corinthians 8:1–2*

. . .I considered all travail, and every right work, that for this a man is envied of his neighbour. This is also vanity and vexation of spirit.

The fool foldeth his hands together, and eateth his own flesh.

Better is an handful with quietness, than both the hands full with travail and vexation of spirit.   *Ecclesiastes 4:4–6*

For when they speak great swelling words of vanity, they allure through the lusts of the flesh. . .   *2 Peter 2:18*

VIGILANCE

We get so busy with our lives that we often forget to concentrate on our relationship with Christ. So many things take up our time, exhausting us, that we often fall into a sort of spiritual snooze. The Bible, however, calls us to be vigilant. It asks that we be wide awake, paying careful attention to what God wants us to do.

Be sober, be vigilant; because your adversary the devil, as a roaring lion, walketh about, seeking whom he may devour:

Whom resist stedfast in the faith. . .

1 Peter 5:8–9

But watch thou in all things, endure afflictions, do the work of an evangelist, make full proof of thy ministry.

2 Timothy 4:5

. . .Awake thou that sleepest, and arise from the dead, and Christ shall give thee light.

Ephesians 5:14

See then that ye walk circumspectly, not as fools, but as wise,

Redeeming the time, because the days are evil.

Wherefore be ye not unwise, but understanding what the will of the Lord is.

Ephesians 5:15–17

Ye are all the children of light, and the children of the day: we are not of the night, nor of darkness.

Therefore let us not sleep, as do others; but let us watch and be sober.

For they that sleep sleep in the night; and they that be drunken are drunken in the night.

But let us, who are of the day, be sober, putting on the breastplate of faith and love; and for an helmet, the hope of salvation.

1 Thessalonians 5:5–8

I will stand upon my watch, and set me upon the tower, and will watch to see what he will say unto me, and what I shall answer when I am reproved.   *Habakkuk 2:1*

And that, knowing the time, that now it is high time to awake out of sleep: for now is our salvation nearer than when we believed.

The night is far spent, the day is at hand: let us therefore cast off the works of darkness, and let us put on the armour of light.

Romans 13:11–12

Behold, I come as a thief. Blessed is he that watcheth, and keepeth his garments, lest he walk naked, and they see his shame.

Revelation 16:15

My heart is fixed, O God, my heart is fixed. . .   *Psalm 57:7*

My soul waiteth for the Lord more than they that watch for the morning: I say, more than they that watch for the morning.

Psalm 130:6

Be watchful, and strengthen the things which remain, that are ready to die: for I have not found thy works perfect before God.

Remember therefore how thou hast received and heard, and hold fast, and repent. If therefore thou shalt not watch, I will come on thee as a thief, and thou shalt not know what hour I will come upon thee.

Revelation 3:2–3

Watch ye, stand fast in the faith, quit you like men, be strong.   *1 Corinthians 16:13*

WISDOM

True wisdom comes not from the world but from heaven.

For Christ sent me not to baptize, but to preach the gospel: not with wisdom of words, lest the cross of Christ should be made of none effect.

For the preaching of the cross is to them that perish foolishness; but unto us which are saved it is the power of God.

For it is written, I will destroy the wisdom of the wise, and will bring to nothing the understanding of the prudent.

Where is the wise? where is the scribe? where is the disputer of this world? hath not God made foolish the wisdom of this world?

For after that in the wisdom of God the world by wisdom knew not God, it pleased God by the foolishness of preaching to save them that believe.

1 Corinthians 1:17–19

And that from a child thou hast known the holy scriptures, which are able to make thee wise unto salvation through faith which is in Christ Jesus.   *2 Timothy 3:15*

And they that be wise shall shine as the brightness of the firmament; and they that turn many to righteousness as the stars for ever and ever.   *Daniel 12:3*

Every wise woman buildeth her house: but the foolish plucketh it down with her hands.
Proverbs 14:1

The law of the LORD is perfect, converting the soul: the testimony of the LORD is sure, making wise the simple. *Psalm 19:7*

But of him are ye in Christ Jesus, who of God is made unto us wisdom, and righteousness, and sanctification, and redemption:

That, according as it is written, He that glorieth, let him glory in the Lord.
1 Corinthians 1:30–31

Who is a wise man and endued with knowledge among you? let him shew out of a good conversation his works with meekness of wisdom.

But if ye have bitter envying and strife in your hearts, glory not, and lie not against the truth.

This wisdom descendeth not from above, but is earthly, sensual, devilish.
James 3:13–15

Wisdom strengtheneth the wise more than ten mighty men which are in the city.
Ecclesiastes 7:19

The fruit of the righteous is a tree of life; and he that winneth souls is wise.
Proverbs 11:30

In the mouth of the foolish is a rod of pride: but the lips of the wise shall preserve them.
Proverbs 14:3

Then shall the kingdom of heaven be likened unto ten virgins, which took their lamps, and went forth to meet the bridegroom.

And five of them were wise, and five were foolish.

They that were foolish took their lamps, and took no oil with them:

But the wise took oil in their vessels with their lamps.

. . .the bridegroom came, and they that were ready went in with him to the marriage: and the door was shut.

Afterward came also the other virgins, saying Lord, Lord, open to us.

But he answered and said. . .I know you not.

Watch therefore, for ye know neither the day nor the hour wherein the Son of man cometh.
Matthew 25:1–4, 10–13

And that from a child hast known the holy scriptures, which are able to make thee wise unto salvation through faith which is in Christ Jesus.
2 Timothy 3:15

Bible Promise Books
for everyone!

only $2⁹⁷

Your days are busy. When is there time for you? When is there a minute to find some peace, to find God? These Bible Promise Books are perfect for busy mothers, fathers, and kids, featuring hundreds of God's precious promises for every day. Arranged in alphabetical order according to subject, God's promises, as recorded in the Bible, are His assurances that He is always with you. Retail $5.95.

Available wherever books are sold.
Or order from:
Barbour Publishing, Inc.
P.O. Box 719
Uhrichsville, Ohio 44683
http://www.barbourbooks.com

If you order by mail, add $2.00 to your order for shipping. Prices subject to change without notice.